Studies of Familiar Birds

STUDIES *of familiar* BIRDS

POEMS BY
Carrie Green

ABLE MUSE PRESS

Able Muse Press

www.ablemusepress.com

Printed in the United States of America

Library of Congress Cataloging-in-Publication Data

Names: Green, Carrie, 1973- author.
Title: Studies of familiar birds / poems by Carrie Green.
Description: San Jose, CA : Able Muse Press, 2020. | Includes bibliographical
    references.
Identifiers: LCCN 2019059840 (print) | LCCN 2019059841 (ebook) | ISBN
    9781773490649 (paperback) | ISBN 9781773490656 (digital)
Subjects: LCSH: Birds--Poetry | LCGFT: Poetry.
Classification: LCC PS3607.R432526 S78 2020 (print) | LCC PS3607.R432526
    (ebook) | DDC 811/.6--dc23
LC record available at https://lccn.loc.gov/2019059840
LC ebook record available at https://lccn.loc.gov/2019059841

Cover image: *Illustrations of the Nests and Eggs of Birds of Ohio (Plates XXIV and
        XXXVIII)*—Jones, Howard; Jones, Virginia Smith; Shulze, Eliza J.

Cover & book design by Alexander Pepple

Carrie Green photo (page 77) by Ayna Lorenzo

Able Muse Press is an imprint of *Able Muse*: A Review of Poetry, Prose & Art—at
www.ablemuse.com

Able Muse Press
467 Saratoga Avenue #602
San Jose, CA 95129

For Mom and Wade

and for my father
Gary Wade Green
1951–2008

Acknowledgments

My grateful acknowledgments go to the editors of the following publications where these poems, some in earlier versions, first appeared:

Arts & Letters: "Some Dreams You Remember" and "Song for My Father" (runner-up, 2013 Arts & Letters Prize for Poetry)

Arts & Letters PRIME: "After the Diagnosis" (runner-up, 2012 PRIME Poetry Prize)

Beloit Poetry Journal: "Green Heron" (*Plate XXVII*), "Black-Capped Chickadee" (*Plate LXVI*), and "Kentucky Warbler" (*Plate LXVII*)

Cave Wall: "House Wren" (*Plate L*) and "Ode to the Purple Martin" (*Plate XXVIII*)

Crab Orchard Review: "The Last Time My Father Left the House" (as "The Last Time My Father Left the House before He Died"), "Rattle," and "First Trip on the St. Martins River after My Father's Death"

DIAGRAM: "Ruby-Throated Hummingbird" (*Plate XXV*, Fig. 1) and "Golden-Winged Warbler" (*Plate LXL*, Fig. 2)

The Drum: "Test Drive"

Flyway: "Portrait of Man as Passenger Pigeon," "Portrait of Young Woman as Red-Headed Woodpecker," and "Portrait of Ornithologist as Short-Eared Owl"

The Heartland Review: "At the Thursby House, Blue Spring State Park"

PANK: "Ode to the Mourning Dove" (*Plate XXIV*) and "Funeral"

Poetry Northwest: "Cliff Swallow" (*Plate XLI*)

Terrain.org: "Study for Long-Billed Marsh Wren," "Long-Billed Marsh Wren" (*Plate XLVI*), and "Field Sketch for Meadow Lark"

Unsplendid: "Robbing the Bees" and "Migration"

"I Wished I Could Knit" appeared in the *2011 Hippocrates Prize for Poetry and Medicine Anthology* (Top Edge Press, 2011) as "When My Father Was Dying, I Wished I Could Knit"

"My Father's Shirts" appeared in *The Cancer Poetry Project 2: More Poems by Cancer Patients and Those Who Love Them* (Minneapolis, MN: Tasora Books, 2013)

"Funeral" is dedicated to the memory of Ennis Whiddon.

Thank you to Alex Pepple for believing in this book.

I am grateful to all who offered comments, friendship, and support during the writing of these poems: A. Van Jordan and friends at the VCFA Postgraduate Writers' Conference, Lisa Russ Spaar and friends at the Kentucky Women Writers Conference, Jennifer Fandel, Kirun Kapur, Lori Larusso, and Jeremy Paden. Thank you to John Wood for knowing I was a poet before I did.

I am indebted to the Kentucky Foundation for Women for a generous grant that made the research and writing of this book possible. Warmest thanks to fellow librarians Kendall Haddix and Joy M. Kiser—to Kendall for introducing me to *America's Other Audubon*, the book that inspired many of these poems, and to Joy for writing it.

My deepest gratitude and love to my family, especially my mother, Pam Green; and brother, Wade Green. Thank you to Ruby for keeping the poems warm. And to my husband, Scott Whiddon: first reader, best friend, best everything.

Contents

III. Unfurl

It is with great sorrow I have to announce to the subscribers to *Illustrations of the Nests and Eggs of Birds of Ohio*, the death, on the seventeenth of last August, from typhoid fever, of my collaborator Miss Genevieve E. Jones.

In the future numbers of the work, [Genevieve's mother] Mrs. Virginia E. Jones will assist with the Illustrations, and the text will be prepared by [Genevieve's brother] Howard E. Jones, A.M., M.D.

—Eliza J. Shulze, 1879

It's only words. But it's words
That bring the beloved back.

—Gregory Orr

I made a god of birds out of the man.

—Katy Didden

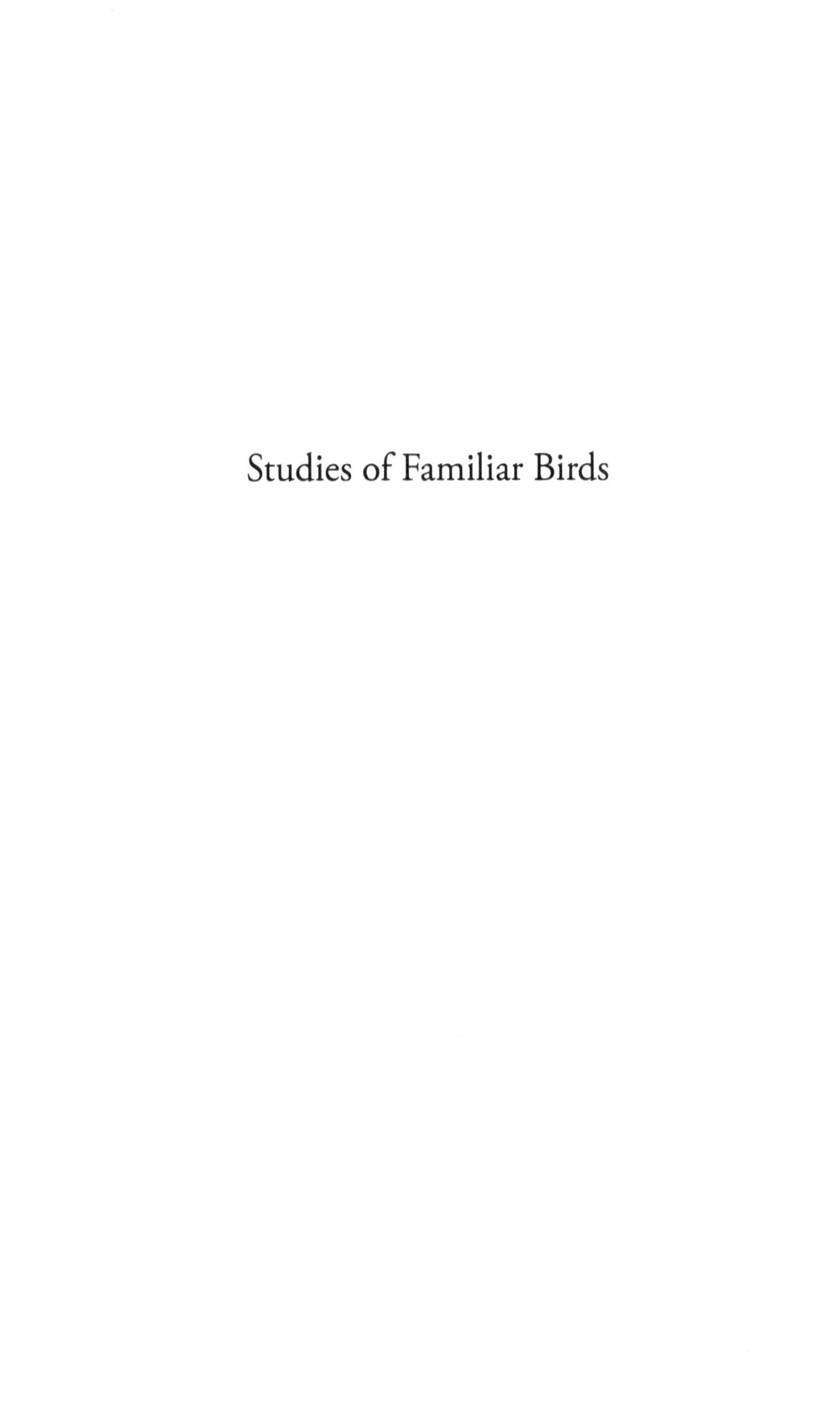

Studies of Familiar Birds

The Studio

You will find it is not enough
        to view the room as panorama.

The clutter of nests and eggs
        blurs beneath a shroud of dust

and all you do not know:
        names, calls, topography.

Not to mention an oriole's wings
        clipping the air beside your ear

or a robin's nest filched
        moments ago and flush

with warm blue eggs. Step inside
        the room. Unlock cabinets

and open drawers to reveal
        the ordered clutches of eggs—

thumb or palm-sized,
        brown as a common hen's

or creamy and swirled like marbles.
        Blown out, insides washed clean.

Unstack the nests from shelves.
    The newspaper packed within

crumbles at your touch. Note
    the yellowed down of willows,

the brittle grasses and weeds,
    and in between

the long gray hair and black thread,
    remnants of someone's mourning.

I. Rattling the Afternoon

At the Thursby House, Blue Spring State Park

Orange City, Florida

When he heard the angels sing,
my father was a child in West Virginia.
There wasn't nobody around, he said,
as we stood beneath a cistern at Blue Spring.

My father was a child in West Virginia
who heard singing above the family cistern.
We stood beneath a cistern at Blue Spring,
the wooden slats stained dark from rain.

He heard singing above the family cistern.
He cried, remembering the angels' hymn
and wooden slats stained dark from rain.
Mom was in the house. The voices came from Heaven.

He cried. Remembering the angels' hymn,
my father peered inside restored rooms.
Mom was in the house. The voices came from Heaven.
A rocking chair wavered behind glass.

We peered inside restored rooms.
There wasn't nobody around, he said.
A rocking chair wavered behind glass.
My father heard the angels sing.

Portrait of Man as Passenger Pigeon

after Aviary (Male Passenger Pigeon/Extinct), *a c-print by*
Sara Angelucci, 2013

The receding line of fair hair suggests
a banker, perhaps a postal clerk,

though he wears no silk or broadcloth tie
to guide us. Only, from the ears down, a skin

of feathers—gray on his face and shoulders,
rust-colored on his right breast and fading

to copper on his left, where the light hits.
Suppose he is on his lunch hour

and entered the studio on a whim,
thinking of his wife. These days,

he has little need for calling cards.
He chooses a white background,

removes his suit and pocket watch,
wanting to be captured without ornament,

as he really is. *To help reveal your strong profile,*
the photographer says, and so he submits

to the posing stand's grip.
Imagine his disappointment

when he sees that his heavy lids
half-obscure his eyes.

The blurred edges of his bust
make him look—already—like a ghost.

Some Dreams You Remember

after Elizabeth Bishop

But their dreams are all inscrutable by eight or nine,
which must be a relief. Better to wake in a haze,
still hearing trains and peacocks calling across fields,
to recall rooms vacant but for chandeliers
swinging, cutting through the humid sadness.
It's bearable, at ten or two, to remember sobbing
but not know why, or to carry the dreams all day
like a pocketful of stones to worry with your thumbs.

How much more preferable than dreams that need
no analysis, dreams you want to forget:
your father's yellowed skin, his body behind glass,
the orange shirt you gave him, shirt you buried him in.
Or, worse, driving him to the hospital and thinking—still,
years later—*he's okay. He's alive. My father didn't die.*

Ode to the Mourning Dove

Plate XXIV, Illustrations of the Nests and Eggs of Birds of Ohio

How can we not love your nests?
Each twig an offering

from male to female
as he stands upon her back.

Such economy, the way the heft
of your bodies molds the sticks.

Spare, we should say, not *crude*,
not *flimsy*. Please forgive us

for finding your tiny heads
so comical above your plump,

delicious breasts. But how we covet
the blue rims lining your black eyes!

And your tranquil coloring—
amid summer's dazzle

of emerald and ruby flight,
we rest our eyes

on the soft grays of your wings,
the rosy buff of your chests.

But mostly we adore
the rattle of wind through your wings,

and how, when dawn's chatter
rises to cacophony,

we can always discern
your throat's pulse.

Oh dove, the sweet ache
of your lament.

Teach us to sing
our grief.

Long-Billed Marsh Wren

*Every ornithologist has noted the fact that but few nests of the
whole number found contain eggs, and many guesses have been
made to account for the construction of so many useless houses.*
   —*Howard Jones* (Plate XLVI)

Impossible,

while considering

    the intricate ribbons of grasses

      lashed to cattails,

the feathers and plant down

    refining the interior,

not to think

    of the other nests—

unlined, emptier

    than husks—

hidden like typhoid in marshes,

    small temples

      to promise

unfulfilled.

House Wren

(Plate L)

The average specimen almost fills
        whatever vessel contains it,
from beehive to mortise,
        amorphous as water.

Here, the nest's base of twigs
        sprawls into a loose pile,

the cup's frothy rim
        of chicken feathers
no longer hiding
        inside the apple tree.

                But surely we all know
                        this nest. We've found it

                in our coffee cans,
                        in our barns and privies—
                inside all our little caves
                        of emptiness, mundane as pockets

                                or a child's boot forgotten
                                        by the back door.

14

Robbing the Bees

after John Wood

Brother, one day the grove and hives will empty:
the neighbor's trees frozen back to stumps,
our father's bees scattered across the scrub.
But today the scent of orange blossom
reaches our patch of sand, and the beeyard
teems with thieving wings. Our father works
the hives, white shirt buttoned to the neck,
hands glove-clumsy. Veiled, he's mysterious

as a bride. Brother, we'll want to recall
the pollen-dusted light kissing scrub oak
and sand pine, the needles smoking in tin,
the bees' stunned flight as our father offers
a taste of honey on his pocketknife.
Our tongues steal sweetness from the rusted blade.

After the Diagnosis

Hontoon Island State Park, DeLand, Florida

We walked the hammock to the shell mound,
my father first on the hard-packed path.
Shadows of palms and oaks slanted like rungs,
the path a shining ladder through trees.

My father led us on the hard-packed path,
head down, sharp elbows swinging. Did he see
the path shining like a ladder through trees?
We followed him through the hush of fronds.

Head down, sharp elbows swinging, did he see
the red lichen bloom like cells on trunks of trees?
We followed him through the hush of fronds
and the trunks' stains, bright as open wounds.

The lichen bloomed like cells on trunks of trees.
The sabal palms curved and leaned,
their red stains bright as open wounds.
Trail ends here. We needed to be told.

A sabal palm curved and leaned
into the wide arms of a dead oak.
Trail ends here. We needed to be told.
The midden sinks into swampy ground.

My Father's Shirts

My father cleared his room the spring
he found out. *So your mother won't have to*, he said,
as he opened the metal doors of the closet
and rattled the quiet afternoon. He plucked shirts
from hangers and held them out to decide
which to toss and which to keep.

He'd paced all morning, needing to keep
himself busy. It was late spring,
but the magnolias hesitated, unable to decide
to unfurl. The doctor said
he still had time. There were so many shirts
packed inside my father's closet.

He stared into the open mouth of the closet
at all the clothes too big to keep:
pants that sagged and bunched, shirts
that swallowed him. The warm spring
sun filtered through leaves and blinds. He said,
It shouldn't be so hard to decide.

Why was it so hard to decide?
Birthdays, trips: all contained in his closet.
Your brother gave me this, he said
of a fishing shirt he wanted to keep.
My throat tight, forgetting spring,
I filled the bags with piles of shirts.

I pictured the racks of thrift-store shirts
and knew my father was right to decide
when he could open the window to spring
and brighten the dim hole of his closet.
Still, I wanted him to keep
everything. *You might wear those again*, I said.

I'll never wear these again, he said,
holding up the blue work shirts
with *Gary* stitched in red. *We'll always keep
those*, I said. It was easy to decide
to put them back, safe inside his closet,
ready to be worn another spring.

He died the next spring. My mother said
it hurt to open his closet. We pressed his shirts
to our faces to decide what to keep.

Blur

In the vacant lot between the oncologist's
and Applebee's, a cat darted out

from behind the fence, a streak of white
stitching the brown grass.

Plump and pink-nosed, she should've been
kneading an heirloom quilt

or tracking the blue flicker of wings
from a windowsill—

not mending the edges
of a four-lane road with her silken coat.

"Do you want to get her?" my father said,
slumping a little in the passenger seat.

This was back when the drugs still worked,
back when driving him to chemo

then waiting for hours beneath the TV's blast
felt like jobs well done. "I don't know."

I was thinking of my own cat, a stray, all the offerings
of tuna before she'd sprung into my lap.

Maybe this cat knew to turn
from the din of engines and wheels.

Then I saw her crouch. The car
was still in gear. We didn't move.

"It's over," my dad said. "She didn't feel a thing.
You couldn't have stopped her."

I want to go back. To open the car door.
To stop her leap off the curb,

the twitch and blur of her small death.

Portrait of Poet as Barn Owl

after Aviary (Barn Owl/Endangered), *a c-print by Sara Angelucci, 2013*

It's tempting to imagine her a spinster aunt
haunting the upper rooms in dotted swiss—

you see it in the widow's peak
and the tawny feathers below her chin,

her face outlined like a white heart.
And in her ear: the bare, meaty lobe.

But then you notice her left eyebrow
arched into a triangle, the black eyes

and golden nib of her beak. Picture her leap
off the ledge into the inky night.

She listens for the rustle and skitter
below leaves and dives down

into a blind strike. Consider her catch,
pinned and writhing. The ruthless

mercy of swallowing it whole.

Praise Song for Wilson's Thrush

(Plate LVIII)

Praise the utility of leaf mold and rootlets, vines and weed stems
Praise the bits of dried leaves scattered like ash across your desk

Praise the mother bird for gathering these remnants
Praise her cinnamon-dusted breast for shaping the cup

Praise the fever that brought you the brown-eyed girl with feathers
　　for hair
Praise her long neck curved above you like a heron's

Praise the father's song, the metallic flourishes that let you hear the
　　emptiness
Praise the echo of dreams carried like notes caught inside a pipe

Praise the blown-out eggs, the balm of turquoise
Praise the clean white rooms inside them. Praise the blank stone.

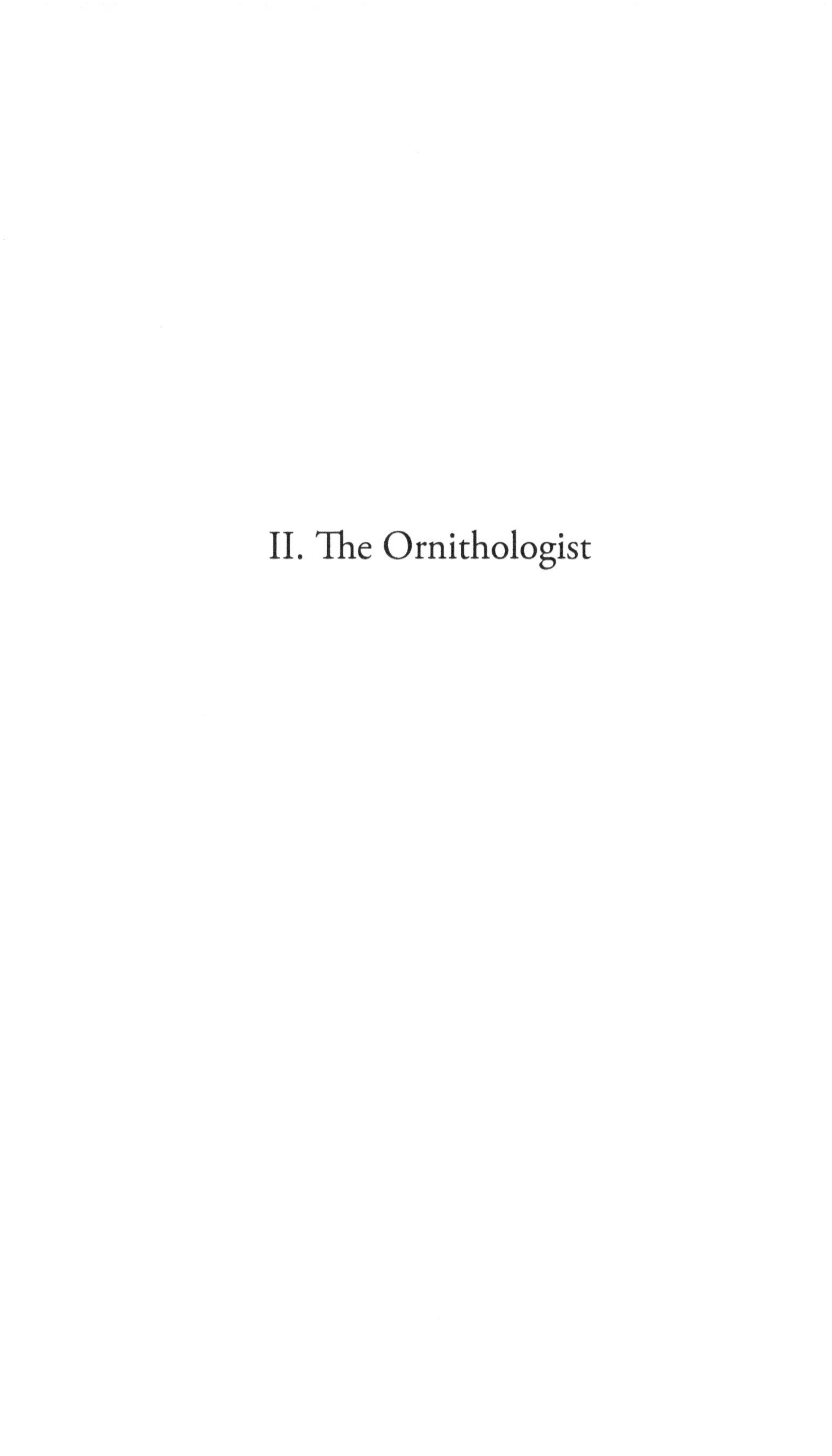

II. The Ornithologist

Loggerhead Shrike

(Plate IX)

after Genevieve's death, Virginia prepares her first lithograph

Nest, crayons, blank stone—
      all as her daughter left them
on her drafting table, even the worktop's height.

Loggerhead Shrike. Embarrassing,
      how little the label means to her.
Perhaps it's best, as she begins,

not to see the small bird
      impaling its prey
but to focus on the crook in the tree—

branch, thorns, leaves—on the tangle
      of twigs and fibers, grasses and weeds.
With each scrape of black wax, she learns

what Genevieve knew: how to weave
      horsehair in weed stems, the fan
of chicken feathers, curl of rootlets,

the fine silk of milkweed.
      How to make an image
shine back at her from stone.

Portrait of Genevieve as a Young Woman

The photograph once pleased Virginia:
the way the light catches in Genevieve's eyes
and burnishes her curls to amber,
how it blanches the stain of her rosacea
to marble. The gold rosette earrings
widen her slim cheeks.
Genevieve made the suit herself—
not with the blue silk Virginia suggested
but with stiff brown tweed,
the only embellishment
a double row of gold buttons.
They march down her bodice
toward the vignette's haze.
Now Virginia can't look at the portrait
without imagining fog
creeping up her daughter's chest and throat.
It smothers her mouth and nose
and dims her eyes,
rising past the soft down at her hairline
to claim every part of her,
even this relic, this trick of light.

Portrait of Girl as Loggerhead Shrike

after Aviary (Loggerhead Shrike/Endangered), *a c-print by Sara Angelucci, 2013*

Though the jeweled arrow placed high
on the girl's head points

at her ear's neat ridges,
it's clear she knows

there is no denying
her heavy black beak.

The center part in her crimped hair
directs the eye

to the tuft of down at its base,
and the angle of her pose

highlights the upper bill's barb-thin hook.
But she has cinched her white ruff

with feathers, as if she could tether
the hunger brimming at her throat.

Note the almond-shaped eyes,
their whites stark against the black mask,

daring the camera to catch her
before it all spills out.

Beneath her shoulders, her body disappears.
If she rose, would she lift up

arms to greet us,
or black and sepia banded wings?

Green Heron

(Plate XXVII)

First she draws the limb, branches stripped
        to gnarled joints.
Then the pile of twigs,
        stark as November

and so brittle she can hear
        the snap. Virginia settles
the familiar curves of eggs
        into the jumble

and admires the lack
        of fibers and feathers—
knowing, as the birds do,
        that you may as well

lay your babies down
        on a bed of bone.

Study for Long-Billed Marsh Wren

Before she finds
the crook and bend
of marsh grass,
Virginia sketches the mass
of yarn and thread
that squats like a tumor
at the bottom of her sewing kit.
A mystery how the skeins
unspool themselves
into snarls, but here
she intwines
the crimson grosgrain
from Genevieve's best dress
with the indigo wool
from her favorite gloves,
as if weaving a spell
for a daughter who loved
to unpuzzle the tangles
of remnants, whether
silk or weed stem,
velvet or vine.

Ode to the Blue Jay

Can there be boldness
without a tilt

toward meanness?
Even your appearance

manifests daring:
the blue crest that rises

at the first slight;
the line of black collar

starched upon the gray breast;
the black bars and white scallops

banding blue wings. Braced
against the scaled trunks of pines,

festooned with thorns,
only the nest's interior betrays

any softness. Who can deny
the audacity as you pilfer rootlets

from our fresh graves?
Take them, little bird.

We need only dirt
to line our final beds.

Study for Ruby-Throated Hummingbird

Virginia breaks the eggs open
with her sketch until two nestlings
spill out, their tiny bodies
hunched like raisins
inside the lichen-plastered nest.

She composes what she recalls:
the sharp triangles of bills,
the bulge of eyes beneath shut lids,
the stringy down along the spine,
awkward as a first mustache.

She documents the birds' imagined growth.
Their beaks lengthen and eyes open.
Their quills prick through black skin.
Then the greening feathers
and wings that strain

against the stretched-out nest.
Virginia fledges the birds
out the studio window to the garden,
where trumpet vine waits
for the flash of still-white throats.

Virginia Recalls the Aviary

Afternoons, she found cheerful tableaux
inside the children's rooms—

the assembled flocks busy
with seed and song,

a hummingbird cradled
in Howard's palm,

an oriole perched
in Genevieve's chestnut hair.

But at dawn the house rang
with notes dissonant

as an orchestra tuning.
So many birds, their competing calls

amplified by walls and windows
and spreading beyond them

like a contagion.

Portrait of Young Woman as Red-Headed Woodpecker

Though her ancestors hollowed out
their homes from dead trees,
she pictures herself in the finest parlor,
poised on a settee, her scarlet head brilliant

against the gold damask wallpaper.
The black fascinator, the drop earrings,
the collar like a gardenia spilling petals
down her white breast—all chosen

to show where she belongs.
Even, she hopes, her hair—
pulled back tight above her ears,
a few tendrils frizzed and loosened

to frame her pale forehead.
She imagines waiting for her suitor,
or suitors, her black and white wings
wrapped around herself like a shawl.

She is listening for the grandfather clock
when the shutter's release brings her back.
You cannot tell if, beneath her red feathers,
her cheeks flush. Her beak points at you

like a knife. She knows where you'd keep her:
beside the corals and conch shells,
the crumbling nests and blown-out eggs,
locked like a specimen behind a glass door.

Ruby-Throated Hummingbird

*In this position, chosen by himself, my hand warmed the little
body until it ceased to live.*
    —*Howard Jones* (Plate XXV, *Fig. 1*)

Hours to measure

    the scale of nest to leaf;

to frill each shingle of lichen;

    to wind each strand of web

around the branches.

    None of it enough

to comprehend

    the palm-sized nest

or death.

Quail

*Here the whole covey was exterminated; but as I felt sorry
for the act, did not intend it, and would never do it again, it
should not be considered unpardonable.*
        —*Nelson Jones* (Plate XVIII)

Pink clover flowers hang
        like pompoms on a curtain of grass,

                open to expose

a crowd of eggs—
        pure white, knuckle-sized—

already preparing, in their incubation,
        for their synchronized lives:

for sleeping tail to tail, ever watchful
        in a plump wreath of birds;

for the dash through open field
        to the cover of pines;

for knowing how close
        to let the dogs sniff

before rising in a clamor
        of gunfire and wings.

Cliff Swallow

(Plate XLI)

Loosed from the barn wall,
        the nest will not keep—
it films worktop and fingertips
        with grime, eager to return

to dust. Virginia defines
        each scallop of dried mud,
constructing, pellet by pellet,
        the gourd-shaped whole.

Her work is nothing
        next to the thousand mouthfuls of mud
ferried and plastered. To guard
        the entrance, she includes a bird,

white forehead and brick throat
        brightening the tunnel.
Note the black beak,
        a pointed arrow, and the body,

a stocky bullet, ready—
        should you try to glimpse
the clutch of dappled eggs—
        to lunge at your thieving heart.

Ode to the Purple Martin

(Plate XXVIII)

Darling Martin, dear chunky swallow—

you never doubt our desire for you.
Your stout neck, your feathers,

gray-brown or black and glossed
with violet. Pugnacious aerialist,

we marvel at your nightly dance
and bet on you against wren

or hawk. You are happy to colonize
whatever box we build for you:

to bustle in columned mansions
or worship in churches,

to fulfill your civic duty
in domed courthouses.

The humblest gourds we hollow—
winter-colored crooknecks, freckled

as some other bird's eggs—
ring with your chortles and croaks.

Even here, on this yellowed print,
you do not question our need

for your face to shield us
from the gourd's stark mouth.

Fever

The quilt Virginia huddles beneath
is too blue—Delft blue, not sky.
It is not her quilt, but it is her quilt.

That window opens too wide—
she's shivering; someone shut it, please.
It is not her window, but it is her window.

And the girl leaning over her—
a slender curving beak
interrupts her face,

and chestnut down blooms
like moss over her skin—
she is and isn't Genevieve.

Don't move, Virginia, don't
startle her. Feel the kiss
of her bill against your cheek.

The feathers trimming her skirt
silence its rustle. She cannot speak,
Virginia, but maybe she will sing.

Brown Thrush

(Plate XXXI)

Virginia stacks the twigs like kindling
       between the hawthorn's forked branches,

each stick absorbing the flame of her attention
       until the nest's shape emerges—

coarse basket for gathering eggs and sky.
       Then she explores the edges:

the chewed leaf, the frayed ends of rootlets,
       one feathery strand of hay.

Behind the nest, she mirrors a cluster
       of thinner, y-shaped branches.

One peeks out at the top, its stem pointing down
       as if to divine the grave;

its opposite escapes at the bottom, stem trailing
       up toward the heavens.

Kentucky Warbler

(Plate LXVII)

As always, Virginia begins
    with what's before her:

the lining's dark swirl
    of rootlets and horse hair,

the rim of vines,
    the foundation of dead leaves.

She closes her eyes to summon
    the sapling keeping watch,

the oak and elm leaves
    decaying on the forest floor,

piled high as the nest,
    circling it like a drain.

It's only after she's added
    three eggs to the center

that she sees the nest
    for what it is:

a tunnel inside her grief,
      the eggs peering up like eyes

from the dust below.

Golden-Winged Warbler

(Plate LXI, *Fig. 2*)

Virginia does not know this bird
       nor wish to see
the ghost of golden crown and wings

alight on the nest.
       It's enough to picture
the damp warmth of leaf litter,

the birch leaf curled like a lid
       over eggs still lit from within.
She reads the raised lines of petioles

like braille, translates ridges
       of grapevine into wax.
Her fingers can barely detect

the pinprick holes
       out of which the blush
of yolk and albumen

leaked.
       Another blanched shell,
while the mother's marks—

wreaths of Vandyke and bistre flecks
       born of her blood—
remain.

III. Unfurl

Funeral

49

If we were crows,
      we'd gather in the trees
and look down at you,

the shock of your body—
      a heap of black feathers,
broken neck and wing—

eased by the veil of leaves.
      We'd call to each other,
our voices rattling

branches and windowpanes.
      Some of us would fly
from tree to tree to make sure

we all understood.
      Perhaps we'd even
scold you a little,

our sentiment as blunt
      as our beaks. We'd know
we couldn't rouse you,

though it would please us
      to sense the mice stirring,
the moles tunneling

deeper below ground
        in your honor.
If not for the trees

beginning to pitch and moan
        beneath our weight,
we could go on and on.

We wouldn't want
        to leave you.
We'd stretch and thin our caws

into silence. Above you,
        our wings would beat the sky,
grief unfurling

        like a shroud.

The Last Time My Father Left the House

In the grove, next year's citrus
hung leaf-green on trees,

and this year's oranges
brightened branches

or the ground where they had fallen.
We should have known

it was too late, the fruit easing
past ripeness.

We should have left them
for the ants and birds.

White blossoms veiled
the scent of sugar

turning. Bees droned
inside the blooms, dizzy

with the promise
of more sweetness.

I Wished I Could Knit

Beneath the green insistence
of hospital lights, I dreamed

thick wool between my fingers,
blue-gray streaked with cream

and enough scratch to know
we were alive. I'd knit a blanket

to cover my father's skinny legs
sticking out from the hospital gown,

to hide his feet in hospital socks,
the soles dotted with sticky pads

like a child's footed pajamas.
In the doctor's waiting room—

tired of flipping through cancer magazines
with their recipes for nourishing

squash soup, TV that nobody watched
blaring—I wished for a ball of cashmere

and busy hands that could whip up
a luxury for the chemo hat donation box.

When folks came over to sit
and stare, I thought the warm click

of wooden needles would shield us
from their mournful eyes.

And keeping watch inside his room,
I longed for the austerity of wool

dyed from bark and berries,
loose coils of marigold and rust.

I'd knit under and around
his ragged breath, twisting it tight

inside each small stitch,
always joining in new skeins—

knit knit, purl purl, Father
Father, never letting

the yarn run out.

Migration

Lake Woodruff National Wildlife Refuge, DeLeon Springs, Florida

I wanted to linger in another country,
far from the hiss of oxygen through tubes,
from my father's skin mottling like bruised fruit.

To know the ease of wind and water—
white pelicans resting on a lake,
a line of bright wings billowing through fog.

Not these reminders—
a pile of bloody fur, a wake of vultures
blocking the path between ponds.

I couldn't hear my breath.

*

I couldn't hear his breath.

Blocking the path between ponds,
a pile of bloody fur, a wake of vultures.
Not these reminders—

a line of bright wings billowing through fog,
white pelicans resting on a lake.
To know the ease of wind and water—

far from skin mottling like bruised fruit,
from the hiss of oxygen through tubes.
I wanted to linger in another country.

Portrait of Ornithologist as Short-Eared Owl

after Aviary (Short-Eared Owl/Special Concern), *a c-print*
by Sara Angelucci, 2013

Trussed upon the posing stand, he eyes
the photographer from behind a mask of feathers.

You cannot be certain of their color,
but the human shape of his eyes suggests

they are neither pale yellow nor sulfur—
amber, perhaps, or olive drab.

If it were up to him, he would record the color
before plucking them from the specimen.

Also, he'd explore the oddity of the bare pate
with his sharpest scalpel.

It's possible his own proclivities prevent him
from trusting the photographer.

Or maybe it's because he cannot move
his head; cannot clap

his downward pointing beak at you;
cannot display the talons

he wants you to know
are there, just out of view.

Test Drive

We walked back to dance camp from lunch
at Hardee's, three fourteen-year-olds proud
that we'd crossed the highway together,

proud of our new Keds gleaming
on legs we'd baked all summer—
legs that could, if we wanted them to,

kick the brims of our costumes' cowboy hats,
flatten our sprayed bangs, and send purple sequins
scattering like falling stars.

Parading down the sidewalk, we dreamed
an audience of ball-capped boys in pickups
craning their necks to stare at us.

I'd like to say that we sensed
the white limo slow beside us
and quickened our pace at the sound

of the tinted window easing down,
but we didn't. "Carrie," a man's voice said,
and, heart marching double time, I turned to see

only my father grinning in his blue mechanic's shirt.
"Wanna ride?" he asked. Then the cold blast
of air conditioning against August's heat.

Our sweaty flesh pimpled and our legs
stuck to gray velvet as we piled
into the wayback. My father couldn't help

but tell us the car belonged
to the funeral home, his eyes crinkling
in the rear view mirror at our squeals,

the box of white tissues tapping my knee,
all of us laughing, fourteen and joyriding
in death's sidecar, oblivious to grief.

Rattle

We were just outside your window
while our mother tended you.
We didn't leave for long,
pacing beneath the magnolia's filtered light.

While our mother tended you,
she soothed with a hum of whispers.
We paced beneath the magnolia's filtered light.
We could still hear your throat rattle

through the hum of our mother's whispers.
It felt good to be outside, drinking tea.
We could still hear your throat rattle.
I read it's the sound of air through water.

It felt good to be outside, drinking tea
and brushing the ruffled tops of petticoat ferns.
The sound of air through water.
The ice melted in my glass.

As I brushed the ruffled tops of petticoat ferns,
whispering turned to sobbing.
The ice melted in my glass,
but I didn't drop it when you died.

Whispering turned to sobbing.
We hadn't left for long.
I didn't drop the glass. When you died,
we were just outside your window.

Field Sketch for Meadow Lark

In a field stained April green,
	her son pointed at the swirl of grass
that signaled the nest.

Virginia glimpsed the eggs glisten
	like wet stones. *Abandoned,*
he said, which took the sting

out of the mother's cries.
	He unstitched the green grass from brown
to expose the nest's dome—

a frame for tiny beaks to bloom like secrets,
	a window opening
into first, staggering flight.

First Trip on the St. Martins River after My Father's Death

Sunset, and sea and sky and river
shimmer like the pearled interior

of shells. The curved backs of dolphins
circle, wet breaths rising, punctuating

silence. It's hard to turn away
from the blaze of pink and orange

behind a city of purple clouds.
My brother steers us back, the boat skipping

over small waves, the sky's color lifting.
The path between the mangroves narrows.

*

Lost, he says after a while, but it's okay
while the sky's still gray. *No names*

on the GPS, he says, *only numbers*,
and we can't find the channel

and our mother can't find the light
though *he always kept it on board.*

Soon my brother's driving blind—
no moon, no stars, just me on the bow

pointing to the vague shapes
of channel markers and hoping to discern

an anhinga perched high on a buoy,
wings spread wide to guide us home.

We can always get out and walk,
Mom says, old joke at a shallow river,

and just as she says it the boat snags
against an oyster bar and sticks so tight

there's no poling it off. *At least we still
have Sea Tow*, Mom says, and then

we wait, cradled by water, anchored
between the dim mounds of mangroves,

the air soft against our skin, a fine mist,
to see how dark the night can be.

Ode to the American Goldfinch

You brighten our doldrums
with reproduction's bustle,

plugging the crooks of thistles
water-tight, rearing your first brood

long after the neighbors have ousted
their second. If we're lucky,

we'll glimpse you dart above us—
flash of sulfur in the green haze—

and pause our constitutionals
to watch you alight on sunflowers.

Their heads bow like benevolent
dinner plates as you tease out

their seeds. From the copse of oaks,
your trills and warbles

flit above the white noise of the cicadas.
You are *the thing with feathers*,

but I haven't made a habit
of you yet. Bird, be still,

just for a moment. Perch above me,
lurid yellow against the dark

face of the sunflower.
Let me get my fill.

Things My Father Said

Will your mother ever have another dog?
Who will take care of this place?
What kind of car will she buy next?
Do you think that you'll have children?

Who will take care of this place?
They haven't said it's cancer.
Do you think that you'll have children?
The Lord could heal me.

They haven't said it's cancer.
If I'm still healthy. If I'm still alive—
the Lord could heal me.
I'm sorry. I can't help it.

If I'm still healthy, if I'm still alive,
I want to see the redwoods.
I'm sorry. I can't help it.
I just think about where I'm going.

I want to see the redwoods.
I hope you'll understand.
I just think about where I'm going
and how good He is to me.

I hope you'll understand
if I don't fight it.
God is so good to me.
I'm at peace with it.

If I don't fight it,
will I be in pain?
I'm at peace with it.
I am trying to tell you.

Portrait of Young Man as Non-Breeding Bobolink

after Aviary (Winter Male Bobolink/Threatened), *a c-print by*
Sara Angelucci, 2013

He poses in his drabbest garments,
the brindled coat he exchanges each year

for spring's flash of black and white.
Perhaps he wants to convey

a sense of purpose, to convince
his sweetheart—maybe even himself—

of his intentions. Observe the white feathers
sharpened into a collar,

the small bill polished to rose-gold.
And the posture: so stiff,

you can feel the cold metal of the posing stand
clamped against your own neck.

It's the swoop of feathered hair
that betrays him, combed off his forehead

into a rakish wave, pointing up
to the blue glass of the skylight

as if poised for flight.

Black-Capped Chickadee

(Plate LXVI)

Virginia eases the stump open along the seam,
    afraid the decaying wood

might collapse upon its secret. Inside,
    even the heartwood crumbles.

She sketches jagged, illegible rings,
    the half moon where the birds first tunneled,

edges sharp as a bite. Her lines cramp
    near the tree's disintegrating core.

Against the wood's striations,
    the nest appears in relief:

a cloud of moss and down
    that holds its shape when released

from the cavity's embrace. A tree's heart
    hardens and dies a little each day.

How lucky, then, to have the dust replaced
    with bits of moss and fur, to begin

again with freckle-spattered eggs.

Song for My Father

Father, let us go and find a country church,
spare and white with snug, hard pews.

We'll drive out in your Ranger—
January's brown fields blurring by,

cassettes rattling across the dash—
and slip into silence like an old coat.

In the gravel parking lot, you'll note
the imprint of the rake's tines,

and I'll find the graveyard's blue roses
almost cheerful. Don't shake your head

at the unlocked door—let's pretend
they were expecting us. Inside,

our breaths mingle with dust motes
on chilly slants of stained-glass light.

We'll sit on the left, a few rows back,
and turn our hymnals to "Blessed Assurance."

I'll follow your voice, high and clear
with that touch of mountain tremolo

that stayed long after you left. Father,
I'll try to hold on as your song

swells the rafters like a rib cage
and thrums inside my hollow throat,

as you hold the notes
far beyond where I can go.

In most cases, I have used the same bird names as the authors of *Illustrations of the Nests and Eggs of Birds of Ohio* (Circleville, OH: 1886), though current nomenclature may have changed.

All Roman-numeral numbered *"Plates"* in the book, listed without further attribution, refer to the corresponding *Plate* in *Illustrations.* . . .

Epigraphs on page xi:

> Genevieve Jones died of typhoid fever at the age of thirty-two, just one month after the book's first plates were mailed to subscribers. Genevieve's family decided to complete the project in her honor, with Genevieve's mother, Virginia—a woman with no experience in scientific illustration—producing the lithographs in Genevieve's place. Genevieve's brother, Howard Jones, wrote the text accompanying each plate.

> The first epigraph is quoted by Howard Jones in "Personal Reminiscences" from the Nelson E. Jones Family Collection, MSS 1349, Ohio Historical Society.

"Study for Ruby-Throated Hummingbird" on page 33: The descriptions of the baby hummingbirds were based on images and text in *Baby Birds: An Artist Looks into the Nest* by Julie Zickefoose (Boston, MA: Houghton Mifflin Harcourt, 2016)

"Quail" on page 38: The epigraph is from *Illustrations of the Nests and Eggs of Birds of Ohio*. Nelson Jones was Virginia's husband and the father of Genevieve and Howard.

"Fever" on page 42: According to Joy M. Kiser, both Virginia and Howard contracted typhoid fever while working on the book. "They recovered," Kiser writes, "but Howard suffered heart damage and Virginia's eyes were permanently weakened" (18, *America's Other Audubon*, New York, NY: Princeton Architectural Press, 2012).

"Golden-Winged Warbler" on page 46: Howard Jones uses the phrase "Vandyke and bistre" in his text.

Other Sources:

> The full text of *Illustrations of the Nests and Eggs of Birds of Ohio* can be found online at archive.org/details/Illustrationsne1Jone and at archive.org/details/Illustrationsne2Jone

> In addition to the information in Howard Jones's notes, I obtained information about birds primarily from the Cornell Lab of Ornithology's website, allaboutbirds.org, and *The Birds of North America Online*.

I also consulted the following works:

> Beals, Sharon. *Nests: Fifty Nests and the Birds That Built Them*. San Francisco, CA: Chronicle Books, 2011.

> Goodfellow, Peter. *Avian Architecture: How Birds Design, Engineer & Build*. Princeton, NJ: Princeton University Press, 2011.

> Hauler, Mark E. *The Book of Eggs: A Life-Size Guide to the Eggs of Six Hundred of the World's Bird Species*. Chicago, IL: University of Chicago Press, 2014.

> Purcell, Rosamond, et al. *Egg & Nest*. Cambridge, MA: Belknap Press of Harvard University Press, 2008.

Carrie Green earned her MFA at McNeese State University in Lake Charles, Louisiana, and has received grants from the Kentucky Foundation for Women, the Kentucky Arts Council, and the Louisiana Division of the Arts. Her poems have appeared in *Beloit Poetry Journal, Poetry Northwest, River Styx, Flyway, Blackbird, Cave Wall, DIAGRAM*, and elsewhere.

Also from Able Muse Press

Jacob M. Appel, *The Cynic in Extremis – Poems*

William Baer, *Times Square and Other Stories;*
New Jersey Noir – A Novel;
New Jersey Noir (Cape May) – A Novel;

Lee Harlin Bahan, *A Year of Mourning (Petrarch) – Translation*

Melissa Balmain, *Walking in on People (Able Muse Book Award for Poetry)*

Ben Berman, *Strange Borderlands – Poems;*
Figuring in the Figure – Poems

David Berman, *Progressions of the Mind – Poems*

Lorna Knowles Blake, *Green Hill (Able Muse Book Award for Poetry)*

Michael Cantor, *Life in the Second Circle – Poems*

Catherine Chandler, *Lines of Flight – Poems*

William Conelly, *Uncontested Grounds – Poems*

Maryann Corbett, *Credo for the Checkout Line in Winter – Poems;*
Street View – Poems
In Code – Poems

John Philip Drury, *Sea Level Rising – Poems*

Rhina P. Espaillat, *And after All – Poems*

Anna M. Evans, *Under Dark Waters: Surviving the* Titanic *– Poems*

D. R. Goodman, *Greed: A Confession – Poems*

Carrie Green, *Studies of Familiar Birds – Poems*

Margaret Ann Griffiths, *Grasshopper – The Poetry of M A Griffiths*

Katie Hartsock, *Bed of Impatiens – Poems*

Elise Hempel, *Second Rain – Poems*

Jan D. Hodge, *Taking Shape – carmina figurata;*
The Bard & Scheherazade Keep Company – Poems

Ellen Kaufman, *House Music – Poems*
Double-Parked, with Tosca – Poems

Emily Leithauser, *The Borrowed World (Able Muse Book Award for Poetry)*

Hailey Leithauser, *Saint Worm – Poems*

Carol Light, *Heaven from Steam – Poems*

Kate Light, *Character Shoes – Poems*

April Lindner, *This Bed Our Bodies Shaped – Poems*

Martin McGovern, *Bad Fame – Poems*

Jeredith Merrin, *Cup – Poems*

Richard Moore, *Selected Poems;*
The Rule That Liberates: An Expanded Edition – Selected Essays

Richard Newman, *All the Wasted Beauty of the World – Poems*

Alfred Nicol, *Animal Psalms – Poems*

Deirdre O'Connor, *The Cupped Field (Able Muse Book Award for Poetry)*

Frank Osen, *Virtue, Big as Sin (Able Muse Book Award for Poetry)*

Alexander Pepple (Editor), *Able Muse Anthology;*
   Able Muse – a review of poetry, prose & art (semiannual, winter 2010 on)

James Pollock, *Sailing to Babylon – Poems*

Aaron Poochigian, *The Cosmic Purr – Poems;*
   Manhattanite (Able Muse Book Award for Poetry)

Tatiana Forero Puerta, *Cleaning the Ghost Room – Poems*

Jennifer Reeser, *Indigenous – Poems*

John Ridland, *Sir Gawain and the Green Knight (Anonymous) – Translation;*
   Pearl (Anonymous) – Translation

Stephen Scaer, *Pumpkin Chucking – Poems*

Hollis Seamon, *Corporeality – Stories*

Ed Shacklee, *The Blind Loon: A Bestiary*

Carrie Shipers, *Cause for Concern (Able Muse Book Award for Poetry)*

Matthew Buckley Smith, *Dirge for an Imaginary World (Able Muse Book Award for Poetry)*

Susan de Sola, *Frozen Charlotte – Poems*

Barbara Ellen Sorensen, *Compositions of the Dead Playing Flutes – Poems*

Rebecca Starks, *Time Is Always Now – Poems*
   Fetch Muse – Poems

Sally Thomas, *Motherland – Poems*

J.C. Todd, *Beyond Repair – Poems*

Paulette Demers Turco (Editor), *The Powow River Poets Anthology II*

Rosemerry Wahtola Trommer, *Naked for Tea – Poems*

Wendy Videlock, *Slingshots and Love Plums – Poems;*
   The Dark Gnu and Other Poems;
   Nevertheless – Poems

Richard Wakefield, *A Vertical Mile – Poems*
   Terminal Park – Poems

Gail White, *Asperity Street – Poems*

Chelsea Woodard, *Vellum – Poems*

Rob Wright, *Last Wishes – Poems*

www.ablemusepress.com